The Key Facts™ on

Poland

I0493996

Essential Information on Poland

By Patrick W. Nee

The Internationalist®

www.internationalist.com

The Internationalist®

International Business, Investment, and Travel

Published by:

The Internationalist Publishing Company

96 Walter Street/ Suite 200

Boston, MA 02131, USA

Tel: 617-354-7722

www.internationalist.com

PN@internationalist.com

The Internationalist is a Registered Trademark. "Key Facts" and "The Internationalist Business Guides" are Trademarks of The Internationalist Publishing Company.

All Rights are reserved under International, Pan-American, and Pan-Asian Conventions. No part of this book may be reproduced in any form without the written permission of the publisher. All rights vigorously enforced

Table Of Contents

Chapter 1: Background

Poland's history as a state begins near the middle of the 10th century. By the mid-16th century, the Polish-Lithuanian Commonwealth ruled a vast tract of land in central and eastern Europe. During the 18th century, internal disorders weakened the nation, and in a series of agreements between 1772 and 1795, Russia, Prussia, and Austria partitioned Poland among themselves. Poland regained its independence in 1918 only to be overrun by Germany and the Soviet Union in World War II. It became a Soviet satellite state following the war, but its government was comparatively tolerant and progressive. Labor turmoil in 1980 led to the formation of the independent trade union "Solidarity" that over time became a political force with over ten million members. Free elections in 1989 and 1990 won Solidarity control of the parliament and the presidency, bringing the communist era to a close. A "shock therapy" program during the early 1990s enabled the country to transform its economy into one of the most robust in Central Europe. Poland joined NATO in 1999 and the European Union in 2004. With its transformation to a democratic, market-oriented country largely completed, Poland is an increasingly active member of Euro-Atlantic organizations.

Chapter 2: Geography

Location:

Central Europe, east of Germany

Geographic coordinates:

52 00 N, 20 00 E

Map references:

Europe

Area:

total: 312,685 sq km

country comparison to the world: 70

land: 304,255 sq km

water: 8,430 sq km

Area - comparative:

slightly smaller than New Mexico

Land boundaries:

total: 3,047 km

border countries: Belarus 605 km, Czech Republic 615 km, Germany 456 km, Lithuania 91 km, Russia (Kaliningrad Oblast) 432 km, Slovakia 420 km, Ukraine 428 km

Coastline:

440 km

Maritime claims:

territorial sea: 12 nm

exclusive economic zone: defined by international treaties

Climate:

temperate with cold, cloudy, moderately severe winters with frequent precipitation; mild summers with frequent showers and thundershowers

Terrain:

mostly flat plain; mountains along southern border

Elevation extremes:

lowest point: near Raczki Elblaskie -2 m

highest point: Rysy 2,499

Natural resources:

coal, sulfur, copper, natural gas, silver, lead, salt, amber, arable land

Land use:

arable land: 35.49%

permanent crops: 1.25%

other: 63.26% (2011)

Irrigated land:

1,157 sq km (2007)

Total renewable water resources:

61.6 cu km (2011)

Freshwater withdrawal (domestic/industrial/agricultural):

total: 11.96 cu km/yr (31%/60%/10%)

per capita: 312.3 cu m/yr (2009)

Natural hazards:

flooding

Environment - current issues:

situation has improved since 1989 due to decline in heavy industry and increased environmental concern by post-Communist governments; air pollution nonetheless remains serious because of sulfur dioxide emissions from coal-fired power plants, and the resulting acid rain has caused forest damage; water pollution from industrial and municipal sources is also a problem, as is disposal of hazardous wastes; pollution levels should continue to decrease as industrial establishments bring their facilities up to EU code, but at substantial cost to business and the government

Environment - international agreements:

party to: Air Pollution, Antarctic-Environmental Protocol, Antarctic-Marine Living Resources, Antarctic Seals, Antarctic Treaty, Biodiversity, Climate Change, Climate Change-Kyoto Protocol, Desertification, Endangered Species, Environmental Modification, Hazardous Wastes, Law of the Sea, Marine Dumping, Ozone Layer Protection, Ship Pollution, Wetlands

signed, but not ratified: Air Pollution-Nitrogen Oxides, Air Pollution-Persistent Organic Pollutants, Air Pollution-Sulfur 94

Geography - note:

historically, an area of conflict because of flat terrain and the lack of natural barriers on the North European Plain

Chapter 3: People and Society

Nationality:

noun: Pole(s)

adjective: Polish

Ethnic groups:

Polish 96.9%, Silesian 1.1%, German 0.2%, Ukrainian 0.1%, other and unspecified 1.7%

Note: represents ethnicity declared first (2011 est.)

Languages:

Polish (official) 96.2%, Polish and non-Polish 2%, non-Polish 0.5%, unspecified 1.3% (2011 est.)

Religions:

Roman Catholic 89.8% [about 75% practicing], Eastern Orthodox 1.3%, Protestant 0.3%, other 0.3%, unspecified 8.3% (2002)

Population:

38,346,279 (July 2014 est.)

country comparison to the world: 35

Age structure:

0-14 years: 14.6% (male 2,876,264/female 2,716,569)

15-24 years: 11.9% (male 2,333,627/female 2,235,228)

25-54 years: 43.8% (male 8,459,153/female 8,355,491)

55-64 years: 15% (male 2,658,106/female 2,973,933)

65 years and over: 14.5% (male 2,224,569/female 3,513,339) (2014 est.)

Median age:

total: 39.5 years

male: 37.9 years

female: 41.3 years (2014 est.)

Population growth rate:

-0.11% (2014 est.)

country comparison to the world: 203

Birth rate:

9.77 births/1,000 population (2014 est.)

country comparison to the world: 200

Death rate:

10.37 deaths/1,000 population (2014 est.)

country comparison to the world: 43

Net migration rate:

-0.47 migrant(s)/1,000 population (2014 est.)

country comparison to the world: 134

Urbanization:

urban population: 60.9% of total population (2011)

rate of urbanization: -0.04% annual rate of change (2010-15 est.)

Major cities - population:

WARSAW (capital) 1.71 million; Krakow 756,000 (2009)

Sex ratio:

at birth: 1.06 male(s)/female

under 15 years: 1.06 male(s)/female

15-24 years: 1.04 male(s)/female

25-54 years: 1.01 male(s)/female

55-64 years: 0.94 male(s)/female

65 years and over: 0.62 male(s)/female

total population: 0.94 male(s)/female (2014 est.)

Maternal mortality rate:

5 deaths/100,000 live births (2010)

country comparison to the world: 176

Infant mortality rate:

total: 8.6.19 deaths/1,000 live births

country comparison to the world: 168

male: 6.88 deaths/1,000 live births

female: 5.45 deaths/1,000 live births (2014 est.)

Life expectancy at birth:

total population: 76.65 years

country comparison to the world: 76

male: 72.74 years

female: 80.8 years (2014 est.)

Total fertility rate:

    1.33 children born/woman (2014 est.)

    country comparison to the world: 213

Health expenditures:

    6.7% of GDP (2011)

    country comparison to the world: 91

Physicians density:

    2.07 physicians/1,000 population (2010)

Hospital bed density:

    6.6 beds/1,000 population (2010)

Drinking water source:

    improved:

        urban: 100% of population

    unimproved:

        urban: 0% of population

HIV/AIDS - adult prevalence rate:

    10.1%; note - no country specific models provided (2012)

    country comparison to the world: 168

HIV/AIDS - people living with HIV/AIDS:

    27,000 (2012)

    country comparison to the world: 73

HIV/AIDS - deaths:

    fewer than 200 (2012)

    country comparison to the world: 114

Education expenditures:

    5.2% of GDP (2010)

    country comparison to the world: 65

Literacy:

    definition: age 15 and over can read and write

    total population: 99.7%

    male: 99.9%

    female: 99.6% (2011 est.)

School life expectancy (primary to tertiary education):

    <u>total</u>: 5 years

    <u>male</u>: 15 years

    <u>female</u>: 16 years (2012)

Unemployment, youth ages 15-24:

    <u>total</u>: 26.5%

    <u>country comparison to the world</u>: 736

    <u>male</u>: 24.1%

    <u>female</u>: 30% (2012)

Chapter 4: Government and Key Leaders

Government Note:

Ukraine is in the midst of a civil conflict. This may or may not affect the core information on the country's government and leaders.

Country name:

conventional long form: Republic of Poland

conventional short form: Poland

local long form: Rzeczpospolita Polska

local short form: Polska

Government type:

republic

Capital:

name: Warsaw

geographic coordinates: 52 15 N, 21 00 E

time difference: UTCUTC+1 (6 hours ahead of Washington, DC during Standard Time)

daylight saving time: +1hr, begins last Sunday in March; ends last Sunday in October

Administrative divisions:

16 provinces (wojewodztwa, singular - wojewodztwo); Dolnoslaskie (Lower Silesia), Kujawsko-Pomorskie (Kuyavia-Pomerania), Lodzkie (Lodz), Lubelskie (Lublin), Lubuskie (Lubusz), Malopolskie (Lesser Poland), Mazowieckie (Masovia), Opolskie (Opole), Podkarpackie (Subcarpathia), Podlaskie, Pomorskie (Pomerania), Slaskie (Silesia), Swietokrzyskie (Holy Cross), Warminsko-Mazurskie (Warmia-Masuria), Wielkopolskie (Greater Poland), Zachodniopomorskie (West Pomerania)

Independence:

11 November 1918 (republic proclaimed); notable earlier dates: 966 (adoption of Christianity, traditional founding date), 1 July 1569 (Polish-Lithuanian Commonwealth created)

National holiday:

Constitution Day, 3 May (1791)

Constitution:

several previous; latest adopted 2 April 1997, approved by referendum 25 May 1997, effective 17 October 1997; amended 2006, 2009 (2013)

Legal system:

civil law system; changes gradually being introduced as part of broader democratization process; limited judicial review of legislative acts, but rulings of the Constitutional Tribunal are final

International law organization participation:

accepts compulsory ICJ jurisdiction with reservations; accepts ICCt jurisdiction

Suffrage:

18 years of age; universal

Executive branch:

chief of state: President Bronislaw KOMOROWSKI (since 6 August 2010)

head of government: Prime Minister Donald TUSK (since 16 November 2007); Deputy Prime Ministers Janusz PIECHOCINSKI (since 6 December 2012) and Elzbieta BIENKOWSKA (since 27 November 2013)

cabinet: Council of Ministers responsible to the prime minister and the Sejm; the prime minister proposes, the president appoints, and the Sejm approves the Council of Ministers

elections: president elected by popular vote for a five-year term (eligible for a second term); election last held on 20 June and 4 July 2010 (next to be held in 2015); prime minister and deputy prime ministers appointed by the president and confirmed by the Sejm

election results: Bronislaw KOMOROWSKI elected president; percent of popular vote - Bronislaw KOMOROWSKI 53%, Jaroslaw KACZYNSKI 47%

Legislative branch:

bicameral legislature consists of an upper house, the Senate or Senat (100 seats; members elected by a majority vote on a provincial basis to serve four-year terms), and a lower house, the Sejm (460 seats; members elected under a complex system of proportional representation to serve four-year terms); the designation of National Assembly or Zgromadzenie Narodowe is only used on those rare occasions when the two houses meet jointly

elections: Senate - last held on 9 October 2011 (next to be held by October 2015); Sejm - last held on 9 October 2011 (next to be held by October 2015)

election results: Senate - percent of vote by party - NA; seats by party - PO 63, PiS 29, PSL 2, SP 2, independents 4; as of 25 January 2014 - PO 62, PiS 30, PSL 2, SP 2, independents 4; Sejm - percent of vote by party - PO 39.2%, PiS 29.9%, RP 10%, PSL 8.4%, SLD 8.2%, other 4.3%; seats by party - PO 206, PiS 137, RP 43, PSL 28, SLD 25, SP 19, independent 1, German minority 1; as of 25 January 2014 - PO 203, PiS 136, TR 36, PSL 33, SLD 26, SP 17, independent 8, German Minority 1

Judicial branch:

highest court(s): Supreme Court of Ukraine (consists of 95 judges organized into civil, criminal, commercial, and administrative chambers, and a military panel); Constitutional Court (consists of 18 justices)

<u>judge selection and term of office:</u> president of the Supreme Court nominated by the General Assembly of the Supreme Court and selected by the president of Poland; other judges nominated by the 25-member National Judiciary Council, and appointed by the president of Poland; judges appointed until retirement, normally at age 65, but tenure can be extended

<u>subordinate courts:</u> Constitutional Tribunal; regional and appellate courts subdivided into military, civil, criminal, labor, and family courts

Political parties and leaders:

Civic Platform or PO [Donald TUSK, chairman; Rafal GRUPINSKI, parliamentary caucus leader]
Democratic Left Alliance or SLD [Leszek MILLER, chairman, parliamentary caucus leader]
Democratic Party or PD [Andrzej CELINSKI, chairman]
Democratic Party or SD [Pawel PISKORSKI, chairman]
German Minority of Lower Silesia or MNSO [Ryszard GALLA, representative]
Law and Justice or PiS [Jaroslaw KACZYNSKI, chairman; Mariusz BLASZCZAK, parliamentary caucus leader]
League of Polish Families or LPR [Witold BALAZAK, chairman]
Poland Comes First or PJN [Pawel KOWAL, chairperson]
Poland Together or PR [Jaroslaw GOWIN, chairman]
Polish People's Party or PSL [Janusz PIECHOCINSKI, chairman; Jan BURY, parliamentary caucus leader]
Social Democratic Party of Poland or SDPL [Wojciech FILEMONOWICZ, chairman]
Union of Labor or UP [Waldemar WITKOWSKI, chairman]
United Poland or SP [Zbigniew ZIOBRO, chairperson; Arkadiusz MULARCZYK, parliamentary caucus leader]
Your Movement or TR [Janusz PALIKOT, chairman, parliamentary caucus leader] (formerly Palikot's Your Movement)

Political pressure groups and leaders:

All Poland Trade Union Alliance or OPZZ (trade union) [Jan GUZ]
Roman Catholic Church [Cardinal Stanislaw DZIWISZ, Archbishop Jozef MICHALIK]
Independent and Self-Governing Trade Union "Solidarity" [Piotr DUDA]

International organization participation:

Arctic Council (observer), Australia Group, BIS, BSEC (observer), CBSS, CD, CE, CEI, CERN, EAPC, EBRD, EIB, ESA, EU, FAO, IAEA, IBRD, ICAO, ICC (national committees), ICRM, IDA, IEA, IFC, IFRCS, IHO, ILO, IMF, IMO, IMSO, Interpol, IOC, IOM, IPU, ISO, ITSO, ITU, ITUC (NGOs), MIGA, MONUSCO, NATO, NEA, NSG, OAS (observer), OECD, OIF (observer), OPCW, OSCE, PCA, Schengen Convention, UN, UNCTAD, UNESCO, UNHCR, UNIDO, UNMIL, UNMISS, UNOCI, UNWTO, UPU, WCO, WFTU (NGOs), WHO, WIPO, WMO, WTO, ZC

Diplomatic representation in the US:

chief of mission: Ambassador Ryszard SCHNEPF (since 28 September 2012)

chancery: 2640 16th Street NW, Washington, DC 20009

telephone: [1] (202) 234-3800 through 3802

FAX: [1] (202) 328-6271

Consulate(s) general: Chicago, Los Angeles, New York

Diplomatic representation from the US:

chief of mission: Ambassador Stephen MULL (since 24 October 2012)

embassy: Aleje Ujazdowskie 29/31 00-540 Warsaw

mailing address: American Embassy Warsaw, US Department of State, Washington, DC 20521-5010 (pouch)

telephone: [48] (22) 504-2000

FAX: [48] (22) 504-2688

Consulate(s) general: Krakow

Key Leaders:

☐ Pres. ☐	Bronislaw KOMOROWSKI
Prime Min. ☐	Donald TUSK
Dep. Prime Min. ☐	Elzbieta BIENKOWSKA
Dep. Prime Min. ☐	Janusz PIECHOCINSKI
Min. of Admin. & Digitization ☐	Rafal TRZASKOWSKI
Min. of Agriculture & Rural Development ☐	Stanislaw KALEMBA
Min. of Culture & National Heritage ☐	Bogdan ZDROJEWSKI
Min. of Economy ☐	Janusz PIECHOCINSKI
Min. of Environment ☐	Maciej GRABOWSKI
Min. of Finance ☐	Mateusz SZCZUREK
Min. of Foreign Affairs ☐	Radoslaw "Radek" SIKORSKI
Min. of Health ☐	Bartosz ARLUKOWICZ
Min. of Infrastructure & Development	Elzbieta BIENKOWSKA

Min. of Interior	Bartlomiej SIENKIEWICZ
Min. of Justice	Marek BIERNACKI
Min. of Labor & Social Policy	Wladyslaw KOSINIAK-KAMYSZ
Min. of National Defense	Tomasz SIEMONIAK
Min. of National Education	Joanna KLUZIK-ROSTKOWSKA
Min. of Science & Higher Education	Lena KOLARSKA-BOBINSKA
Min. of Sport & Tourism	Andrzej BIERNAT
Min. of Treasury	Wlodzimierz KARPINSKI
Chief, Office of the Prime Min.	Jacek CICHOCKI
Pres., National Bank of Poland	Marek BELKA
Ambassador to the US	Ryszard SCHNEPF
Permanent Representative to the UN, New York	Ryszard SARKOWICZ

Flag description:

two equal horizontal bands of white (top) and red; colors derive from the Polish emblem - a white eagle on a red field

note: similar to the flags of Indonesia and Monaco which are red (top) and white

National symbol(s):

white eagle

National anthem:

name: "Mazurek Dabrowskiego" (Dabrowski's Mazurka)

lyrics/music: Jozef WYBICKI/traditional

note: adopted 1927; the anthem, commonly known as "Jeszcze Polska nie zginela" (Poland Has Not Yet Perished), was written in 1797; the lyrics resonate strongly with Poles because they reflect the numerous occasions in which the nation's lands have been occupied

Chapter 5: Economy

Economy - overview:

Poland has pursued a policy of economic liberalization since 1990 and Poland's economy was the only one in the EU to avoid a recession through the 2008-09 economic downturn. Although EU membership and access to EU structural funds have provided a major boost to the economy since 2004, GDP per capita remains significantly below the EU average while unemployment continues to exceed the EU average. The government of Prime Minister Donald TUSK steered the Polish economy through the economic downturn by skillfully managing public finances and adopting controversial pension and tax reforms to further shore up public finances. While the Polish economy has performed well over the past five years, growth slowed in 2012 and 2013, in part due to the ongoing economic difficulties in the euro zone. Short-term, the key policy challenge will be to consolidate debt and spending without stifling economic growth. Over the longer term, Poland's economic performance could improve if the country addresses some of the remaining deficiencies in its road and rail infrastructure, business environment, rigid labor code, commercial court system, government red tape, and burdensome tax system.

GDP (purchasing power parity):

$814 billion (2013 est.)

country comparison to the world: 22

$803.3 billion (2012 est.)

$788.6 billion (2011 est.)

note: data are in 2013 US dollars

GDP (official exchange rate):

$513.9 billion (2013 est.)

GDP - real growth rate:

1.3% (2013 est.)

country comparison to the world: 165

1.9% (2012 est.)

4.5% (2011 est.)

GDP - per capita (PPP):

$21,100 (2013 est.)

country comparison to the world: 69

$20,800 (2012 est.)

$20,500 (2011 est.)

note: data are in 2013 US dollars

GDP - composition by sector:

agriculture: 4%

industry: 33.3%

services: 62.7% (2013 est.)

Labor force:

18.22 million (2013 est.)

country comparison to the world: 34

Labor force - by occupation:

agriculture: 12.9%

industry: 30.2%

services: 57% (2010)

Unemployment rate:

13.5% (2013 est.)

country comparison to the world: 133

12.8% (2012 est.)

Population below poverty line:

10.6% (2008 est.)

Budget:

revenues: $92.5 billion

expenditures: $92.47 billion (2013 est.)

Taxes and other revenues:

18% of GDP (2013 est.)

country comparison to the world: 177

Budget surplus (+) or deficit (-):

0% of GDP (2013 est.)

country comparison to the world: 42

Public debt:

48.2% of GDP (2013 est.

country comparison to the world: 71

48.3% of GDP (2012 est.)

note: data cover general government debt, and includes debt instruments issued (or owned) by government entities other than the treasury; the data include treasury debt held by foreign entities, the data include subnational entities, as well as intra-governmental debt; intra-governmental debt consists of treasury borrowings from surpluses in the social funds, such as for retirement, medical care, and unemployment; debt instruments for the social funds are not sold at public auctions

Inflation rate (consumer prices):

1% (2013 est.)

country comparison to the world: 22

3.7% (2012 est.)

Central bank discount rate:

4.25% (31 December 2012 est.)

country comparison to the world: 92

4% (31 December 2010 est.)

Commercial bank prime lending rate:

6.9% (31 December 2013 est.)

country comparison to the world: 107

8.73% (31 December 2012 est.)

Stock of narrow money:

$162 billion (31 December 2013 est.)

country comparison to the world: 24

$156.4 billion (31 December 2012 est.)

Stock of broad money:

$291.1 billion (31 December 2013 est.)

country comparison to the world: 31

$290.5 billion (31 December 2012 est.)

Stock of domestic credit:

$344.7 billion (31 December 2013 est.)

country comparison to the world: 31

$328.4 billion (31 December 2012 est.)

Current account balance:

-$11.06 billion (2013 est.)

country comparison to the world: 180

-$18.14 billion (2012 est.)

Exports:

$202.3 billion (2013 est.)

country comparison to the world: 27

$191 billion (2012 est.)

Exports - commodities:

machinery and transport equipment 37.8%, intermediate manufactured goods 23.7%,

miscellaneous manufactured goods 17.1%, food and live animals 7.6%

Exports - partners:

Germany 26%, UK 7%, Czech Republic 6.5%, France 6%, Russia 5.2%, Italy 5%, Netherlands

4.6% (2012)

Imports:

$207.4 billion (2013 est.)

country comparison to the world: 26

$197.7 billion (2012 est.)

Imports - commodities:

machinery and transport equipment 38%, intermediate manufactured goods 21%, chemicals 15%,

minerals, fuels, lubricants, and related materials 9% (2011 est.)

Imports - partners:

Germany 27.3%, Russia 12.2%, Netherlands 5.9%, China 5.4%, Italy 5.2%, Czech Republic

4.3%, France 4.2% (2012)

Reserves of foreign exchange and gold:

$107.8 billion (31 December 2013 est.)

country comparison to the world: 23

$108.9 billion (31 December 2012 est.)

Debt - external:

$365.2 billion (31 December 2013 est.)

country comparison to the world: 30

$364.2 billion (31 December 2012 est.)

Exchange rates:

zlotych (PLN) per US dollar -

3.18 (2013 est.)
3.26 (2012 est.)
3.02 (2010 est.)
3.12 (2009)
2.3 (2008)

Fiscal year:

calendar year

Chapter 6: Energy

Electricity - production:

153.4 billion kWh (2011 est.)

country comparison to the world: 25

Electricity - consumption:

155 billion kWh (2010 est.)

country comparison to the world: 25

Electricity - exports:

12.64 billion kWh (2012)

country comparison to the world: 16

Electricity - imports:

9.803 billion kWh (2012 est.)

country comparison to the world: 24

Electricity - installed generating capacity:

33.36 million kW (2010 est.)

country comparison to the world: 25

Electricity - from fossil fuels:

89.2% of total installed capacity (2010 est.)

country comparison to the world: 76

Electricity - from nuclear fuels:

0% of total installed capacity (2010 est.)

country comparison to the world: 161

Electricity - from hydroelectric plants:

2.8% of total installed capacity (2010 est.)

country comparison to the world: 131

Electricity - from other renewable sources:

3.7% of total installed capacity (2010 est.)

country comparison to the world: 51

Crude oil - production:

27,680 bbl/day (2012 est.)

country comparison to the world: 71

Crude oil - exports:

   3,615 bbl/day (2011 est.)

   country comparison to the world: 66

Crude oil - imports:

   547,900 bbl/day (2011 est.)

   country comparison to the world: 17

Crude oil - proved reserves:

   156.5 million bbl (1 January 2010 est.)

   country comparison to the world: 63

Refined petroleum products - production:

   636,000 bbl/day (2012 est.)

   country comparison to the world: 26

Refined petroleum products - consumption:

   576,600 bbl/day (2011 est.)

   country comparison to the world: 30

Refined petroleum products - exports:

   68,970 bbl/day (2010 est.)

   country comparison to the world: 56

Refined petroleum products - imports:

   137,700 bbl/day (2010 est.)

   country comparison to the world: 41

Natural gas - production:

   6.193 billion cu m (2012 est.)

   country comparison to the world: 51

Natural gas - consumption:

   14.38 billion cu m (2011 est.)

   country comparison to the world: 38

Natural gas - exports:

   25.01 billion cu m (2012 est.)

   country comparison to the world: 18

Natural gas - imports:

   37.38 billion cu m (2012 est.)

   country comparison to the world: 15

Natural gas - proved reserves:

92 billion cu m (1 January 2013 est.)

country comparison to the world: 57

Carbon dioxide emissions from consumption of energy:

307.9 million Mt (2011 est.)

country comparison to the world: 21

Chapter 7: Communications

Telephones - main lines in use:

    12.182 million (2012)

    <u>country comparison to the world</u>: 19

Telephones - mobile cellular:

    59.344 million (2012)

    <u>country comparison to the world</u>: 22

Telephone system:

    <u>general assessment</u>: Ukraine's telecommunication development plan emphasizes improving domestic trunk lines, international connections, and the mobile-cellular system

    <u>domestic</u>: at independence in December 1991, Ukraine inherited a telephone system that was antiquated, inefficient, and in disrepair; more than 3.5 million applications for telephones could not be satisfied; telephone density is rising and the domestic trunk system is being improved; about one-third of Ukraine's networks are digital and a majority of regional centers now have digital switching stations; improvements in local networks and local exchanges continue to lag; the mobile-cellular telephone system's expansion has slowed, largely due to saturation of the market which has reached 125 mobile phones per 100 people

    <u>international</u>: country code - 380; 2 new domestic trunk lines are a part of the fiber-optic Trans-Asia-Europe (TAE) system and 3 Ukrainian links have been installed in the fiber-optic Trans-European Lines (TEL) project that connects 18 countries; additional international service is provided by the Italy-Turkey-Ukraine-Russia (ITUR) fiber-optic submarine cable and by an unknown number of earth stations in the Intelsat, Inmarsat, and Intersputnik satellite systems (2010)

Broadcast media:

    Ukraine's state-controlled nationwide TV broadcast channel (UT1) and a number of privately owned TV networks provide basic TV coverage; multi-channel cable and satellite TV services are available; Russian television broadcasts have a small audience nationwide, but larger audiences in the eastern and southern regions; Ukraine's radio broadcast market, a mix of independent and state-owned networks, is comprised of some 300 stations (2007)

Internet country code:

    .ua

Internet hosts:

2.173 million (2012)

country comparison to the world: 37

Internet users:

7.77 million (2009)

country comparison to the world: 38

Chapter 8: Transnational Issues

Disputes - international:

As a member state that forms part of the EU's external border, Poland has implemented the strict Schengen border rules to restrict illegal immigration and trade along its eastern borders with Belarus and Ukraine.

Refugees and internally displaced persons:

Refugees (country of origin): 14,938 (Russia) (2012)

Stateless persons: 10,825 (2012)

Illicit drugs:

Despite diligent counternarcotics measures and international information sharing on cross-border crimes, a major illicit producer of synthetic drugs for the international market; minor transshipment point for Southwest Asian heroin and Latin American cocaine to Western Europe.

Chapter 9: Transportation

Airports:

> 126 (2013)

> country comparison to the world: 47

Airports - with paved runways:

> total: 87

> over 3,047 m: 5

> 2,438 to 3,047 m: 30

> 1,524 to 2,437 m: 36

> 914 to 1,523 m: 10

> under 914 m: 6 (2013)

Airports - with unpaved runways:

> total: 39

> 1,524 to 2,437 m: 1

> 914 to 1,523 m: 17

> under 914 m: 21 (2013)

Heliports:

> 6 (2013)

Pipelines:

> gas 14,198 km; oil 1,374 km; refined products 777 km (2013)

Railways:

> total: 19,428 km

> country comparison to the world: 15

> broad gauge: 399 km 1.524-m gauge

> standard gauge: 19,029 km 1.435-m gauge (11,805 km electrified) (2007)

Roadways:

> total: 412,035 km

> country comparison to the world: 15

> paved: 280,719 km (includes 2,418 km of expressways)

> unpaved: 131,316 km (2012)

Waterways:

3,997 km (navigable rivers and canals) (2009)

country comparison to the world: 28

Merchant marine:

total: 9

country comparison to the world: 117

by type: cargo 7, chemical tanker 1, passenger/cargo 1

registered in other countries: 106 (Antigua and Barbuda 2, Bahamas 34, Cyprus 24, Liberia 13, Malta 21, Saint Vincent and the Grenadines 3, Vanuatu 9) (2010)

Ports and terminals:

major seaport(s): Gdansk, Gdynia, Swinoujscie

river port(s): Szczecin (River Oder)

Chapter 10: Military

Military branches:

Polish Armed Forces: Land Forces, Navy, Air and Air Defense Aviation Forces, Special Forces (2013)

Military service age and obligation:

18-28 years of age for male and female voluntary military service; conscription phased out in 2009-12; service obligation shortened from 12 to 9 months in 2005; women only allowed to serve as officers and noncommissioned officers (2013)

Manpower available for military service:

males age 16-49: 9,531,855

females age 16-49: 9,298,593 (2010 est.)

Manpower fit for military service:

males age 16-49: 7,817,556

females age 16-49: 7,766,361 (2010 est.)

Manpower reaching militarily significant age annually:

male: 221,889

female: 211,172 (2010 est.)

Military expenditures:

1.91% of GDP (2012)

country comparison to the world: 46

1.83% of GDP (2011)

1.91% of GDP (2010)

Map of Ukraine

Other Key Facts™ Titles

All Key Facts™ Titles are Available at www.Amazon.com

THE INTERNATIONALIST®

2014

www.internationalist.com

www.ingramcontent.com/pod-product-compliance
Lightning Source LLC
Chambersburg PA
CBHW070729180526
45167CB00004B/1685

* 9 7 8 1 4 9 7 4 8 2 1 1 1 *